EXPLORING
THEATER

Costume Design in Theater

Ruth Bjorklund

Cavendish Square
New York

Published in 2017 by Cavendish Square Publishing, LLC
243 5th Avenue, Suite 136, New York, NY 10016

Library of Congress Cataloging-in-Publication Data

Names: Bjorklund, Ruth.
Title: Costume design in theater / Ruth Bjorklund.
Description: New York : Cavendish Square Publishing, 2017. | Series: Exploring theater |
Includes index.
Identifiers: ISBN 9781502622778 (library bound) | ISBN 9781502622785 (ebook)
Subjects: LCSH: Costume—Juvenile literature. | Theater—Juvenile literature.
Classification: LCC PN2067.B56 2017 | DDC 792.02'6--dc23

Editorial Director: David McNamara
Editor: Fletcher Doyle
Copy Editor: Nathan Heidelberger
Associate Art Director: Amy Greenan
Designer: Jessica Nevins
Production Coordinator: Karol Szymczuk
Photo Research: J8 Media

CONTENTS

In the famous musical *Cats*, the challenge for costume designers was transforming all the actors into cats.

CHAPTER ONE

HAVING WHAT IT TAKES

The curtain goes up and the action begins. The audience sits back to relax, enjoy, and be entertained. Meanwhile, the people onstage and the people backstage have been working at a frenzied pace designing, rehearsing, and collaborating. Besides actors learning lines and taking stage directions, theater troupes also prepare scenery, lighting, sound, props, and costumes. The costumes? Costumes are not created simply by operating a sewing machine. Costume designers must interact with every part of the production and employ a variety of skills and techniques. Costume designers interact with stage managers, set designers, sound and lighting engineers, and the actors themselves to get a clear idea of their responsibilities to the production.

Vision

Costume designers require many skills and talents to be successful. Foremost, costume designers must be capable of vision, or understanding the big picture. On the other hand, costume designers must also be capable of carrying out the smallest details.

What natural talents do people have that can lead them to understand the scope of the role of a costume designer? People are attracted to the job in order to explore their interests in many fields, such as drawing, fashion design, drama, **textiles**, jewelry making, sewing, and more. Not every person considering taking on the job of costume designer needs to be an expert in every aspect of the role, but it is important for each to develop a thorough knowledge of the fundamentals.

A costume designer renders some early design ideas to present to the play's director.

Communication

Costume designers must have good communication skills. They need to be very familiar with the script and be able to grasp the essence of the characters in order to communicate with the other theater members involved in technical production. Costume designers begin by absorbing the workings of the production—sets, scripts, characters, lighting, and so on. Once the costume designer has studied the actors and the production needs, he or she must have the verbal, as well as technical, skills to communicate design ideas clearly.

What skills are useful in communicating costume designs? There are numerous technical skills involved in costume design, but starting with a basic appreciation for theater history, literature, music, and dance is the foundation for communicating costume design with others. Sharing knowledge and the enjoyment of the theater arts enables all members of the troupe to better interact.

Costume designers also need to show leadership ability. In most productions, the costume designer will manage a team. Sometimes, there is a costume assistant and/or a group of volunteers and interns. In other situations, there may be many departments that a costume designer will oversee: the costume shop, where the costumes are made; the wardrobe department, which keeps inventory of the costumes, prepares them for the actors backstage, and repairs, cleans, and stores the costumes; and sometimes hair and makeup stylists.

Rendering

For a costume designer, a basic skill is the ability to draw, or render, an idea or concept. **Rendering** is not an exact reproduction of the costume but rather an interpretation of the costume. Many costume designers make use of design software, such as Adobe Photoshop, Corel Draw, or software created specifically for costume or fashion designers. But there are just as many costume designers who prefer to sketch their designs by hand, using colored pencil or watercolor. Some designers use a combination of skills—sketching by hand and digital drawing. Many also sketch their designs and then scan them into a design program, allowing them to quickly make changes to things such as color or fabric **texture.**

Design renderings are not detailed drawings but rather sketches that suggest how a costume or garment will fit or how it will look as the character moves about. While many designers draw figures well, some do not, but that does not put them at a major disadvantage. For those who do not opt for computerized drawing, many use body outline sheets, called **croquis**. Croquis templates come in a variety of body shapes, positions, and angles.

Crafting the Costume

After the design and rendering stage, costume designers draw on their crafting skills. Designers draft and cut out patterns, machine stitch, hand stitch, paint and dye fabric, tailor, glue, and embellish their garments. They also fashion hats and other headpieces, such as masks, helmets, or wigs. Sometimes a costume requires specially designed shoes or other footwear. Many fantasy and science fiction productions call for specialized additions, such as wings, horns, spines, or tails. Costume designers also design and fabricate jewelry.

A key skill to develop is **draping**. Draping uses inexpensive fabric, such as muslin. After drawing the pattern, the costumer cuts it out in sections using the muslin. The muslin pattern pieces are then pinned onto a dressmaker's dummy to form an example of the shape and style of the garment.

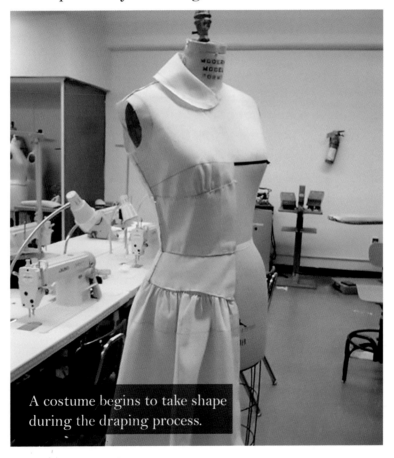

A costume begins to take shape during the draping process.

Other Skills

Besides having the skills to create and make art, a costume designer needs to have the ability to organize. Theater work is often very hectic, and a different deadline seems to loom each day. A costume designer has to know how to schedule costume and wardrobe staff (if there is a staff), director's meetings, actors' fittings, shopping excursions, vendors' calls, and more, all the while making sure there is an adequate amount of time for actual design work.

Record keeping is another organizational task that needs to be done with concise detail. Designers keep files that contain information on how the costumes are constructed, the materials used, and how to care for and store costumes. Designers have to keep track of each individual costume—when it is worn, how it is worn, and by whom, together with any accessories, jewelry, and personal props that go with the clothes. Costume designers also record where the costume and its accessories are stored and where they will be located backstage during the performance. Every item must be carefully labeled and put into inventory. Many scenes call for groups of people or crowds, and there is individual paperwork for each of those costumes and costume changes as well. Although scheduling record keeping may seem too time consuming in the course of a busy day, many different people—costume and wardrobe staff, the director, and the actors—will rely on the information.

Near the top of any list of skills needed by a costume designer is the ability to work with a specific, and usually a very tight, budget. Managing money is a major responsibility. Nearly all costume decisions require budget considerations. Should this costume be made or rented? Can a less costly fabric be used? Is it possible to add or take away accessories in order to make a costume appear different in another scene, or is a new costume necessary? How much of the budget should be set aside to pay for any unexpected or last minute costume needs? Expecting the unexpected is a very necessary skill. Finding solutions and being flexible are musts, as is being able to work well under pressure. This pressure comes not only from deadlines but from the needs of the other members of the theater company.

Research

Research skills are essential to designing and developing costumes. Designing, rendering, and crafting costumes are the outward display of costume design, but none of it can happen without serious time spent on research. Many begin their research by looking at costume books and theater and film books and magazines. Very often the costume designer is given the script in the early part of the production so that he or she has the time to study the script, think, and do research. A valuable form of research is attending plays and movies, as well as viewing paintings on exhibit in museums and galleries, all the while paying special attention to the costuming.

To get a broad background of costuming, check out illustrated books about historical eras, other cultures, and special dress styles. Some examples include:

- Ancient societies, such as Greek, Mayan, or Egyptian

- Ethnic dress, such as West African, Peruvian, Hindu, Native American, Polynesian, or Inuit

- Historic, such as Shakespearean, Roaring Twenties, Chinese, or Persian

- Special groups, such as military, religious, or fantasy figures

Practice

Practice in making costumes is the best way to decide whether or not costume design is a good fit for you. Drawing and sketching develops rendering skills. It is always a good idea to carry around a sketch pad or notebook. Spend a little time each day sketching.

Sewing well is a fundamental skill for a costume designer.

Scroll through books and magazines for interesting figures or garments to copy. Given extra time, such as on weekends, try to take some time drawing in more detail and using colored pencils or watercolors. Understanding how colors work together is key for a costume designer.

There are many how-to craft books on patternmaking, hat making, and jewelry making. There are books that teach the art of sewing, from machine sewing elaborate ball gowns or superhero costumes to smaller tasks such as making button holes or stitching on fringe. There is no need to spend a lot of money buying new fabric and **trim** when practicing patternmaking and sewing. Shop at thrift stores and buy used clothes, sheets, bedcovers, or curtains to cut up and reuse.

Through practice, many people find they are attracted to a certain style or skill. Some may find that tailoring men's clothing is satisfying, others may prefer historical costumes. Some people discover they enjoy fabric finishing. There are many craft books and magazines that focus on textiles. Painting, dyeing, and otherwise surface treating (such as **distressing** a fabric to make it look old) require a lot of steps and take a lot of practice.

After designing and constructing a few costumes from scratch, choose a play with a minimal amount of characters and costume changes and try to design costumes for all the characters in the play. The job of a costume designer is to create an overall impression, and the best way to practice doing so is designing a collection of costumes. Costumes in a play should relate to one another, by being either coordinated or dramatically in contrast.

Extra Activities

Most high schools have art classes, and many community programs offer classes to the public in drawing, sewing, and jewelry making. Artists often teach private drawing classes. Many sewing stores, fabric shops, and arts and craft shops also hold demonstrations and classes. One of the most entertaining but time consuming and exhausting parts of the costume designer's job is shopping. Shopping might seem easy, but actually, it can be a challenge. To experience how shopping plays its important role, make a plan to create a few costumes for a play and see what items can be found that might be useful, or could be altered to be useful. It is not necessary to buy anything on these shopping excursions, but visiting department stores, specialty clothing shops, small boutiques, and thrift stores, and taking notes or snapping photos is a good way

While having a vast variety of material options, costume designers must carefully and creatively narrow their choices.

to practice. Examine how garments are made and what details are interesting. Consider different ways the garments could be dyed, painted, altered, decorated, or broken down into usable sections. Be sure to take notes and try making quick sketches while at the store. Good costume designers do not copy directly from other designers' work, even if they are designing for the same play. However, costume designers are inspired by each other's work, which is why looking at books, magazines, and the internet, or attending plays and seeing movies, is very helpful.

Visit arts and crafts shops and fabric stores often. It is important to become familiar with the tools of the trade, such as needle sizes and types; different types of thread, cording, and yarn; measuring tools such as hem rulers and measuring tapes; sewing machine attachments; and other sewing notions—beads, sequins, padding, elastic, zippers, snaps, magnets, and buttons. Get to know different types of sewing machines—machines that do basic stitches, sergers, or high-end computerized machines that can do dozens and dozens of stitch types.

If the high school has a drama department, becoming part of the technical crew and doing costume design and construction would be fun and beneficial. There are also many community theaters that would appreciate the services of someone willing to help with costumes, sewing, and wardrobe. Some larger cities have theater troupes that offer internships. They often offer little or no pay, but they are nonetheless valuable and provide enormous on-the-job learning opportunities, besides being a rewarding experience.

A creative team uses art, technology, and a lively exchange of ideas to get a production up and running.

CHAPTER TWO

THE CREATIVE TEAM

The role of the costume designer is quite varied and quite complicated. The costume designer is responsible for the overall look and feel of the costumes and reports directly to the director of the production. Once a play and its director are chosen, the next step is to assemble a **creative team**. The initial team includes the costume designer, set designer (sometimes called the production designer), and if the play contains music and dance, a music director and a choreographer. All of these roles require research, creative thought, and teamwork in order to produce a successful play.

Working with the Director

The director is the hub of the production, and the costume designer is an essential spoke. Together, they work to establish how the visual impact of costumes will add to the audience's appreciation of the play. They begin by discussing time period, color, style, and mood. Mood is the feeling and atmosphere that the play presents—in other words, how the play will make the audience feel. Although the actors' words and movements present the mood, the costume designer's contributions to creating mood are very important. Time period is another principal consideration. The director may want to see a traditional representation of a certain time period or may want the costume designer to tweak the style to create a different interpretation of the play. Color is key to the discussion, as color helps reveal a character's personality or temperament, such as muted colors for a meek character and bold colors for a dominant character. Style will be coordinated closely with time period and setting. After many conversations, the costume designer shows the director his or her sketches, **mood boards**, **look books**, and **tear sheets** to make sure that he or she is understanding the director's aims and vision. A mood board is a collage that communicates the look and feel of a costume, such as color **swatches**, sketches, and fabric samples. The mood board describes the character's costume using terms such as elegant, funny, aggressive, romantic, historic, or frightening. A tear sheet is a collection of examples of possible design ideas torn from magazines, newspapers, or images downloaded from the internet. A costume designer's look book is a collection of photographs of costumes used in other performances.

Working with the Set Designer

The physical look and feel of the production are the decision of the director, who then hands the task of creating the look and feel over to the costume and set designers. The set designer and costume designer together create the mood and emotion of the play and emphasize the historical or geographic setting for the play. The set designer and costume designer use visual elements to engage and inform the audience. The director and the designers work together to decide whether the set should be realistic or abstract. They can opt for historical, realistic, fantasy, or traditional sets, which will influence the costume designer's approach to the costumes. The costume designer and set designer need to work closely so that the costumes and the set are complementary.

It is their job to work together to visually communicate to the audience the emotions, status, or motivations of the characters. For instance, characters who are part of a crowd or do not have speaking roles would likely wear costumes that are inconspicuous.

The costumes fit the mood for the play *Les Misérables*.

Main characters have costumes that more actively interact with the set. During lively scenes, sets may be bold and colorful, and so might the costumes. Quiet scenes may call for muted colors on the part of both the set and costume designers. The set designer, costume designer, and director need to decide whether the set should be colorful or monotone, and if the set will be colored, they must choose a palette—bright primary colors or muted colors, such as pale yellow, rose, or tan. Once that decision has been made, work between the designers must focus on how the set colors and the costume colors interact. Once color and mood have been established, the costume designer and set designer are free to explore their creativity. The director needs the set designer and the costume designer to understand one another in order for each of them to move forward, and that is why it is so important to get the design team together early.

Lighting

The set designer and costume designer also work together to decide how to interact with the lighting director. The set designer, costume designer, lighting director, and director will discuss how light is treated on stage—will it be bright, dim, in shadows, or from spots? For example, if a character is onstage alone and is performing a monologue, the lighting director will often opt for a spotlight. The set designer would likely use for background a set that is low key and unassuming to allow for the actor to literally take center stage. The costume designer must understand the mood of the monologue and choose either a dramatic costume that would stand out under the lights and against the set, or a simple, unassuming costume that would reflect a somber or sad mood. Set designers, costume designers, and lighting designers combine forces to suggest historical period, time of day, weather, and other parts of the play that are not verbally expressed in the script but are necessary to understanding the story line.

Working With Wardrobe

The wardrobe department is often considered part of the costume department. The two departments work together closely but have different responsibilities. The wardrobe department is in charge of the costumes backstage and is responsible for inventory, cleaning, ironing, and mending. The costume designer and his or her staff guide the wardrobe staff. They instruct the wardrobe staff about which costumes are worn by whom and in what order. They also show

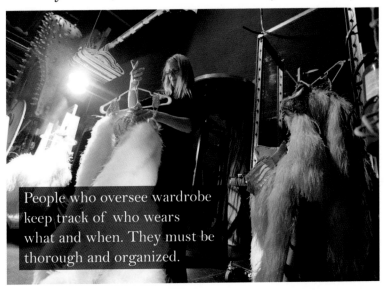

People who oversee wardrobe keep track of who wears what and when. They must be thorough and organized.

the wardrobe staff how to put on the costumes. The wardrobe staff will give feedback to the costume department, advising them if there is any difficulty in doing costume changes efficiently. This can happen if a costume is too complicated to be put on in the time allowed for a particular costume change.

Working With Actors

One of the most important and sometimes very complicated relationships is between the costume designer and the actors and their characters. The costume designer creates the costume for the character, but then must also create the costume to best suit the actor. The designer discusses how the actor perceives the role, and that input helps guide the designer. Actors also have their own feelings about how they wear clothes—opinions about comfort, freedom of movement, or color choice, for example. Another challenge for a costume designer doing historical costumes is that the bodies of people today are different from bodies in times past. Many women are now slimmer, and many men are bigger, so period costumes must be adapted to seem historically correct while still fitting the wearer.

Going Big

In large productions, costume designers must be effective and resourceful managers. They create the designs and oversee the work of others in the department. As the costume department team leader, costume designers give instructions to assistants, shoppers, and technicians. In a big production, the costume designer maintains creative control and interacts with the director and the set, makeup, sound, and lighting designers. He or she researches styles and settings, determines fabrics and other materials, and delegates practical work to assistants and technical staff.

Very large theater groups, such as the Oregon Shakespeare Festival in Ashland or the Huntington Theater Company in Boston, have large budgets and many specialized crew members. The costume designer collaborates with the team leaders of the various costume technical crews. These technical teams include drapers, tailors, pattern cutters, pattern drafters, **costume craft artisans**, wigmakers, painters

Costume craft designers build or modify items such as hats, masks, armor, and jewelry.

and dyers, **stitchers**, costume **fitters**, shoppers, costume rental managers, wardrobe personnel, business office staff, and budget managers.

In many large and medium-sized productions, costume designers rely heavily on assistant costume designers. The costume designer's assistant helps in countless ways, especially as more and more costume designers are called upon to manage budgets, supervise other departments, and communicate repeatedly with accountants, directors, producers, and other creative-department heads. The most effective assistants understand the designer's vision and way of doing things. By earning the designer's trust, assistants have more freedom to shop, help design, and oversee costume construction. Others in the costume department often come to the assistant first to solve problems, such as running out of fabric or handling last minute costume change requests. Ken Van Duyne, a costume assistant, said that his boss taught him "a lot about working with kindness, and how it's a collaborative job—not only between the director and the actor—but it's also a collaborative process with the crew."

Small Scale

In smaller productions, such as the ones done at your school, the costume designer may not only design the costumes and shop for the costumes, but will often make the costumes, too. A costume designer in smaller productions manages a tight budget. A small costume department will find just a few people taking on most of the work. In this case, a costume designer with a small staff, often composed of volunteers, provides or oversees the practical labor—patternmaking and cutting, sewing, and other practical tasks such as knitting, weaving, ironing, cleaning, and mending. Many times in smaller productions, the costume designer will also oversee, or provide, makeup and wardrobe management.

It Never Stops

A theater production begins somewhat calmly—the creative team discusses the script and their individual interpretations of the script. They exchange ideas and communicate regularly while considering what they each will produce. However, once they share a common understanding of the direction the play will take, the pace quickens. Costume designers and their staff must determine costume needs and quickly start shopping and constructing. Several deadlines have to be met, and people rely on others getting their jobs done in order to complete their own. For example, the designer, or the person in charge of selecting the types of fabric, must do so before shopping for the fabric. The designer must relay the costume design so that the patternmaker and cutter can begin. The person who will iron the costume during the sewing process must do the job quickly in order for work to continue. Shoppers who are buying premade garments need to make their selections in a timely fashion so that they can be altered, trimmed, and accessorized. All costumes need to be in very advanced stages and able to be worn in the final week before the play opens, as these rehearsals are full-dress or tech-dress.

When shopping, costume designers take notes and keep a sketchbook handy.

Starting Out

There are many jobs and internships that may help advance your understanding of costume design. A person may be talented, but it takes work to move forward in this field. There are several options for those who want to get practical experience. First, you can volunteer for a lesser role on the costume crew for your high school production. One way to see if you have an interest in costume design is to become and apprentice to tailors or dressmakers, or to work in a clothing store, jewelry store, or for a clothing manufacturer. Taking a job in a beauty salon will help you get an understanding of hairstyling and makeup. People can also benefit by working for a dry cleaner and learning how to clean and handle garments. Probably the most helpful jobs to find are those in fabric or arts and crafts stores.

It is common for people involved in costume design to have started in an entry-level job. You don't need formal training to work on your high school show, just interest. If you are interested in pursuing a job in costume design, it is best to attend a vocational school, community college, or university to increase your chances for employment. Art, theater, costume, and fashion design classes and programs are demanding. Students must be prepared to study as well as spend long hours in hands-on practice.

Time

The hours required of the costume designer can be very long, especially the last week before the show. Expect to work some weekends and evenings. As much as possible, plan school work or a job to fit the production schedule. People must make sacrifices and forego last minute invitations, such as tickets to a concert. If there are previous plans, such as a family vacation, the director needs to know about them from the start. Being part of a theater production is a commitment that should be honored because so many others are depending on you.

Costumes should reflect the
personality of the character
and be historically accurate.

CHAPTER THREE

BEHIND THE SCENES

Costumes are key in bringing characters in a play to life. The heart of the costume designer's job is to express visually the physical, psychological, and emotional status of the characters. "Clothing is communication," costume designer Jonna Hayden told the *Eugene Weekly*. "There's nothing onstage on any actor that's not a choice. It should always explain who the actor is and enhance the story." Costume designers, along with set designers, play central roles in providing the visual cues that help the characters tell the story.

Costume design takes in the elements of color, shape, and texture. Although a costume has a main color, how that color is highlighted or contrasted with other colors draws interest and helps create the character. A costume with contrasting colors, such as blue and gold, will create more of a stir, or tension, than a costume with similar colors such as dark blue and purple. A costume designer determines shape based on who the character is and how the character acts. If the character makes many small, timid, quiet movements, the designer may opt for a figure-hugging type garment that moves only when the character moves. On the other hand, if a character makes exaggerated or sweeping movements, the designer may want to create a costume that flows—a fluttery skirt or baggy pants, for example. The costume designer also uses texture to create interest. Fabric texture affects how light hits the fabric and reflects off of it. If the costume designer wants to spotlight a feature of the costume, he or she will use a shiny or high-contrast texture. If the costume designer wants some part of the costume to stay in the background, he or she would use a flat texture such as canvas or wool. Many designers use contrasting textures because even without color, textures can achieve a great effect, such as a gray wool coat with a shiny gray satin lapel. Although the coat and lapel are the same color, the sheen of the satin stands out against the wool and sends a subtle message to the audience that the wearer is likely wealthy or stylish.

Costume designer Joe Zingo said in the *Eugene Weekly* story, "Costuming is a set of skills, design is a set of skills, knowing color, fabric, and texture is a set of skills. You have to know what a fabric will do, under stress, movement, when it's dyed or distressed. You have to know whether it will suggest wealth or poverty."

On the Job

Most costume designers are self-employed. When the opportunity to design costumes for a play comes their way, they assess the scope of the project and decide how to assemble a team, whether from their own staff or by hiring others, in order to be most efficient. Different productions have different needs and budgets. No matter if the staff is a staff of one or is a large and specialized staff, costume designers are responsible for more than artistry. They must have good communication skills and maintain an even temper while working with a variety of personalities. Besides designing and constructing costumes, costume designers must be able to manage budgets, contracts, deadlines, and the entire costume crew.

Costumes include anything that the performers wear and, on occasion, touch, including clothing, jewelry, footwear, hats, accessories, and sometimes certain props, makeup, hairstyling, and wigs. The responsibilities of the costume and wardrobe staff can be divided into preproduction, production, and postproduction phases. Preproduction includes designing, purchasing, and constructing costumes. The production phase includes last minute preparations, final rehearsals, wardrobe organization and repair, and sometimes makeup and hairstyling. Postproduction is basically "closing up shop," and it includes how the costumes will be handled after the show's run has ended.

The Script

The first step for a costume designer in preproduction is a meeting with the director and other members of the creative team, usually the set designer and the lighting and sound directors. The director presents the script and relates his or her ideas and feelings about the play. Each member of the creative team makes note of when, where, and how his or her expertise and contributions will be needed. The director and the creative team meet several times to discuss the script and their individual interpretations. Eventually, a "shared vision" is formed and the creative team begins working on their individual designs.

The costume designer reviews the script with the creative team to form a shared vision.

Asking the Right Questions

After reading the script, costume designers reread it several times while asking themselves dozens of questions. In order to understand the play, its theme, tone, and characters, they will want to know:

- What is the plot?

- How many acts and scenes?

- What are some of the themes in the play? (e.g., danger, pride, friendship)

- What is the style of the play? (e.g., realism, romanticism, fantasy)

Some scripts make it clear how costumes should look, such as Henrik Ibsen's *Brand*, which calls for bloodied and bedraggled characters.

- What does the physical action of the play call for? (e.g., playing chess, being in a rock band)

- Are there any references to clothing in the text? (e.g., *Girl with a Pearl Earring*)

- Are there any textual references that mention a character is dressed certain way? (e.g., covered in blood)

- What kind of body does the character have?

- How does he/she walk? Sit? Gesture? Stand?

Time and Place

Generally, the first element a costume designer considers is the time period. The play may be contemporary, meaning it is taking place in the present, or it may take place in a period which is referred to as modern, meaning within the last few decades. For both of those instances, a costume designer can often save money and time by buying ready-made garments. To some extent, especially in smaller productions, the minor and walk-on characters can even wear their own clothes or borrow clothes from other people. Ready-made clothing can be bought in clothing stores for many of the characters in contemporary plays. Plays taking place in modern times require more sleuthing. Modern-dress period and "retro" clothing, such as bold stripes from the 1970s or suits with big shoulder pads from the 1980s, are more likely found in second-hand or thrift stores. Costume designers browse old magazines such as 1960s issues of *Vogue* or J.C. Penney catalogs for inspiration. Store-bought costumes are often altered, not only to provide more interest on stage but to make the costume fit the actor properly. In small productions, the costume designer and/or the assistant will do the shopping, altering, and constructing. In large productions, there may be assistants and designated shoppers, but most costume designers really prefer to shop themselves. Given the ability to purchase rather than make costumes, the costume designer will need more shoppers and fewer patternmakers and stitchers.

If the period is historical, costume designers summon up their cultural knowledge to gain awareness of the period. They research family structure, marriage customs, types of government, politics, and economics, as well as what forms of art, music, and literature were popular. Plays can also blend historic and contemporary time periods.

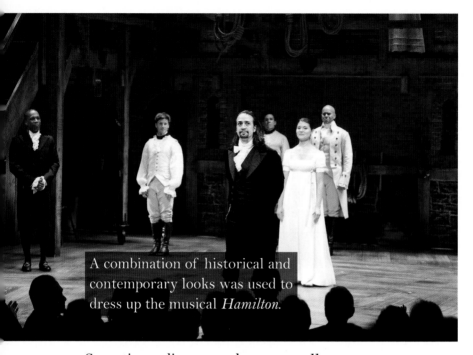

A combination of historical and contemporary looks was used to dress up the musical *Hamilton*.

Sometimes directors choose to tell a contemporary story with characters from the past, or vice versa. Sometimes the director chooses to set the play in a different place or time from the original script. This can be challenging for costume designers as they are often asked for designs that reflect both time periods. For example, a costume designer charged with creating costumes for a historic play in a contemporary setting may dress characters in contemporary clothing but add accessories or alter garments to reflect the past, such as a dress with a long row of tiny buttons, or one with an empire waistline and a hemline shorter in front than back (to suggest a gown with a train), or a man's shirt with loose or slightly blousy sleeves. In the Broadway musical *Hamilton*, the costume designer, Paul Tazewell, mixed eighteenth-century American history with contemporary looks. In some scenes, the male actors wear military clothing—breeches, vests, and boots, but without the traditional adornments of military medals and big brass buttons and chains. But to add a contemporary motif, Tazewell left the actors' heads without historic adornment—no wigs or hats. Rather, the actors wear their own looks—a bun; a ski cap; long, wavy hair.

Taking In the Character

After initially studying the setting, plot, and other elements of the script, the costume designer zeroes in on the characters. Designer Walter Peterson gives this advice: "You have to know how the actor and the director see the character before you can dress them. Once you have an idea of who you're dressing, then you can begin to develop a look that can portray that character." Style and color give information about the character—personality, status, background, mood, and more. The questions designers ask will guide them toward appropriate and character-revealing costumes. Designers should always want to know, what is the character's:

- Age?

- Social status?

- Financial situation?

- Occupation?

- Education?

- Nationality?

- Present home?

- Relationship status?

- Attitude toward others?

- Moral code?

- Personality type?

- Health?

- Mental state?

Designer Judith Bowden explains, "I take my cues from the characters and their surroundings as written in the play, as well as from the stylistic choices of the production. In the same way that an actor builds upon the framework of traits and actions of his or her character in the story, I read what the character does and says for clues about what

The costumes for *Wicked* clearly help the audience identify the characters.

Designing

It all starts with the costume designer, who, besides creating the look and style of each costume, also needs to choose colors, trim, fabric, and fabric treatment (such as dyeing). The people performing the tasks rely on one another. For instance, the designer and patternmaker design the pattern pieces. However, in order to gauge how each pattern piece will fit together, the designer must have already chosen the fabric because the weight

In many plays, background characters wear costumes that bear some relation to each other. Building these garments from scratch is often the designer's best choice.

and texture of the fabric will influence how the pattern is made. Meanwhile, the person who is in charge of finding and purchasing the fabric may not find the right fabric, or enough fabric, or may discover it is too costly. Under such circumstances, the designer and the patternmaker must literally go back to the drawing board.

Measuring

In order to be precise and consistent with measurements, the same person should measure each actor. The best way to measure for a costume is to tie a ribbon around the person's waist and measure up, down, and outward from there. It is important to measure correctly as any alterations that have to be done later because of an incorrect measurement waste time and money. In the largest theater companies, more than fifty measurements are taken for each actor.

Fabrics

Costume designers and people who make fabric selections have to be very resourceful. Theater costume designers and crews rarely buy from general purpose retail fabric stores. Usually, conventional dressmaking fabrics are not bold enough to be used onstage. Colors and textures need to stand out onstage. Large cities, such as Los Angeles and New York, have garment districts where all manner of fabrics can be found. It is not uncommon for costume designers who do not live in a large city and have a fair-sized budget to go on a buying trip to their favorite garment district. High schools rarely have such large budgets, so the ingenuity of a good costume designer can create expensive-looking costumes without expensive fabrics. However, costumes should not be made out of cheap, flimsy materials, as they must withstand the rigors of movement on stage, cleaning, and handling, as well as survive to be reused. Upholstery fabrics, which are durable and often available in strong patterns, are popular. When the costume designer chooses the fabrics and the colors, and the costumes are completed, they may appear to be crude or too flashy when observed up close. Yet that shows the ability of a good costume designer to know how to make a costume bold enough to have an impact on people sitting in the back of the theater. In the same vein, a good costume designer will choose colors that seem garish in normal light but appear natural under stage lights.

When choosing fabrics, costume designers look at color, texture, and durability.

Fabric Specialists

Many wonderful costumes have been created out of basic fabrics and materials. Fabric dyers, painters, and costume craft artisans are inventive, highly valued members of the costume crew. If the costume designer requires a certain pattern or color, fabric dyers and painters can reproduce it. Computer technology in the form of digital fabric printers has given costume designers exciting new options for fabric designs and selection. Although they are expensive to purchase and need careful upkeep, fabric printers can print elaborate and complicated designs on all types of fabric with ease. Costume designers can also send their original pattern designs to fabric-printing companies. A plus in this process is that many characters, especially background characters, can be linked by wearing the same print but in different garment and fabric types—for example, a pattern of swirls and dots can be printed onto wool socks, silk bowties, cotton shirts, and such. Manufacturing technology can produce fabrics that are embroidered, layered, or fused (such as sequins or metallic fibers fused to fabric). These fabrics were once costly and very labor intensive to create.

Painters and dyers treat fabrics to make the costumes look realistic and not unnaturally new. The process is called either distressing or **breaking down**. There are distressing/break-down kits for fabrics available, but many costume designers have their own favorite methods, including rubbing the fabric on cheese graters, belt sanders, nail files, concrete sidewalks, and applying spray paint. There are

Designers all have favorite ways of distressing, or breaking down, fabric to make the costumes appear old and worn.

numerous other techniques to break down fabric, such as smearing the fabric with shoe polish or soaking the fabric in tea or coffee to give it an old, yellowed look. One designer commented that his two favorite methods are burying the fabric in the dirt or running it over with a car. These are costuming tricks that will easily fit into a high school budget.

Finished costumes are also broken down. Shirt sleeves are soaked in water and then tied up with string overnight to create natural looking wrinkles. Pockets are filled with rocks to make them sag. In a production of the play *Annie*, the costume designer described her technique for costuming the orphan girls: "Every single piece of clothing was built, over-dyed, manipulated, torn, then re-sewn, patched, and embroidered to have the look of hand-me-downs."

Costume Craft Artisans

Many wonderful costumes and accessories have been created out of simple and unusual materials.

All variety of unexpected materials have been used to great success. Styrofoam is chief among them, as well as coffee filters, twist ties, netting, drinking straws, plastic bags, wood, papier-mâché, sponges, liquid latex, bric-a-brac, steel, and more. As it is, there is a growing movement to encourage theater costume designers and makers to use recycled materials whenever they can. Costume craft artisans, which also include milliners (hatmakers) and cobblers (shoemakers), make headpieces, handbags, hats, helmets, armor, jewelry, crowns, canes, parasols, fans, lace, swords, shoes, boots, and fantastical appendages such as masks, wings, horns, flippers, fins, and tails.

Draping, Patternmaking, and Stitching

"Draping is the most important part of costume design," believes costume designer Rose Mackey. Draping is a process of draping and pinning fabric onto a dressmaker's dummy padded to the contours of the actor who will wear the costume. The draping process begins by making all sections of the garment (e.g., front of skirt, sleeve, collar, etc.) out of inexpensive material—usually cotton muslin. Muslin comes in a variety of weights, and it is important to choose one that is similar to the costume's fabric. This allows the costume designer to see how the garment falls. Then the sections are draped, positioned, and pinned together. The costume designer will often change the structure of the costume numerous times during draping. After draping, the fabric is removed and used to create the final pattern.

Patterns have traditionally been made by hand, but

Whether costumes are ready made or built, tailors take numerous measurements to fit the costumes to each actor.

many people now use CAD (computer-aided design) software to design patterns. Patternmakers take careful notes, whether the patterns are made by hand or on a computer, so that they can easily redesign or remake the patterns. Some smaller theater groups base their patterns on store-bought paper patterns. Pattern cutters follow the pattern but make large seam allowances so that changes can be made easily when the garment is fit to the actor. The pattern then is **basted** and again fit to the actor (large theater companies have specialized fitters and tailors). Once the costume designer is satisfied, the costume is sewn by stitchers. Often the wide seam allowances are left in the costumes so that the costumes can be fitted to other actors later on.

Stitchers follow the exacting requirements of the patterns and are responsible for seeing to it that the garments are durable. School and community theater plays have short runs, but very successful professional plays can run for months or years. The clothes must also stand up to frequent handling, such as when actors nearly rip off their costumes during costume changes. Costumes are subjected to washing or dry cleaning frequently; in some productions it is done every day. Most elaborately built and rented costumes are not easily or inexpensively cleaned, so many costume designers line expensive costumes with inner shields that can be removed and washed (actors do a lot of sweating under those bright lights). The inner shield adds to the costume's durability. Rarely will a costume designer call for a garment to fasten with zippers or buttons as it is too easy for an actor to fumble with them during a costume change. Some costume designers choose snaps or Velcro, although Velcro is rough and can damage the fabric. Many costume designers opt for magnets to hold the costumes together. After stitchers have finished the construction, the costume is passed along to the costume crafters to provide embellishments.

Shopping for Ready-Made Costumes

Shopping is not all fun and games; it can be very exhausting as well as challenging. Large companies have shoppers or costume design assistants who spend an enormous amount of time in department stores, boutiques, thrift stores, costume shops, craft stores, and even private garage sales. These can be great places for high school designers to come up with inexpensive garments. The challenge is finding clothes that both coordinate with the costume design scheme and come in the right size. Most ready-made costumes will end up being embellished, accessorized, and altered to suit the costume design. Shoppers need to be good record keepers of their activities— they record receipts and price estimates, carry along fabric swatches, costume plots, mood boards, sketches, actors' measurements, and photographs or drawings of set designs. They take copious notes as well as photographs. Shoppers and costume designers look for more than garments: they look for thread, trim, and notions (such as Velcro or snaps), as well as shoes, hats, belts, cufflinks, jewelry, and more. Many costume designers will spot and purchase an intriguing garment or collection of garments or accessories that may be useful in a future production. "A costume designer is a bit of a hoarder," says Sandy Bonds, professor of costume design at the University of Oregon, "an organized hoarder."

Actors Have Their Say

For many reasons, there must be cooperation between actors, costume designers, and the costume crew. Although the costume designer determines the look and style of the costume, the actor must feel comfortable wearing it. Some costume designers say that when they have actors first try on a costume, many of the actors will not look at themselves in the mirror but rather walk, sit, dance, and bend without looking, just to feel if the costume fits right. In productions with many actors and many costume changes, costume designers have their hands full

GO, LINDA CHO!

Linda Cho's mother was an artist who knew firsthand the challenges of making a living in art. When Cho said she wanted to study fine art and design,

Linda Cho designs for many Shakespeare and opera companies. Her costumes are known for being elaborate but easy for actors to wear.

her mother resisted and encouraged her to study medicine. Her mother warned her that as an Asian woman, the likelihood of finding success in the arts was slim.

The conversation continued until Cho's mother relented and Cho flew to Paris to attend the Paris American Academy for a semester. She spent the days at sidewalk cafes, sketching passersby. Returning home to Canada, she studied at McGill University and received a degree in psychology. Although the degree pleased her mother, Cho could not get art out of her head. She took classes in costume construction and joined the Montreal Shakespeare in the Park theater company as an intern.

Cho continued to seek work as a costume designer. She took classes at the Yale School of Drama and designed for numerous college productions. Although she has a novel sense of design, Cho acknowledges that her training in psychology gives her an advantage in understanding a play's characters. "It's not just shopping for cute clothes," Cho says. "It's deciding who these people are." For *A Gentleman's Guide to Love and Murder*, set in Edwardian England, Cho designed historical costumes with a twist— bright colors and quirky trims—and she won a **Tony Award** for costume design. Since then, she has designed for numerous theater productions—from *Ghosts of Versailles* for the Los Angeles Opera to *Peter Pan* for the Children's Theatre Company in Minneapolis.

trying to be sure garments fit well while satisfying the design scheme.

Costume designers involve the actors with as much decision-making as possible and should ask in advance if actors have any allergies to specific fabrics or materials, such as latex or lamb's wool. On occasion, actors may disagree with the costume's design, and compromises have to be reached. Sometimes actors dislike their costumes and feel that they do not represent the character they are trying to develop. This can be a tricky situation and difficult to handle. For example, an actor may say that his or her character would not wear a garment that is cut as short as the design calls for, or the actor might feel personally uncomfortable with the length. Costume designers would appreciate that kind of feedback as they have a responsibility to the production to enhance the character and support the actor. When an actor tries on a costume for the first time, costume designer Kerry Hulson says, "It's the first time we see the shape in three dimensions and on the actual bodies—the bodies determine a lot about how the clothes are cut in the end. It's not just about period accuracy, it's much more about how it looks on the actor … We also have a lot of discussions with the actors during fittings. They have a real sense of how they wear the clothes and the costumes really impact their performances, how they stand, how they move, etc."

Costume designers stay in contact with the actors from the very beginning to try to avoid any snafus later in the costuming process. They attend rehearsals to see how the actors move about the stage. Clothing affected people's posture during the period in which it was worn; designers need to see if costumes force actors to move or sit in a way that is not authentic. They take note of which scenes the actor is called upon to perform physical actions such as kicking, jumping, pushing, dragging, or sword fighting. They also pay attention during costume changes. If there are rapid costume changes, the costume designer needs to be sure the costumes are easy to get in and out of. Sometimes the solution is to layer the costumes, so the next costume is worn underneath the first costume. Another method for a quick change is to design the costume so the actor can walk into it arms first and be fastened in the back, by a wardrobe assistant or another cast member, rather than having the actor put the costume on over his or her head. Costume designers do not produce their final costumes until the costumes fit the actor's physique and the actor feels comfortable.

The Fit

All costumes, whether store bought or built, are fit on the actor, at least two or three times. During fittings, the costume designer, fitter, or tailor will take several measurements and photographs. Costume designers, tailors, fitters, and stitchers must expect to be flexible in making changes and alterations. As the production moves forward, both director and costume designer will make adjustments to the costumes' design and style. Changes can be made because of a last-minute design change, a change in the script, or to refit the actor. Sometimes the actor will have gained or lost weight, or found through performing in rehearsals

Costumes can go through numerous changes and repairs—sometimes just moments before the actor goes onstage.

that the costume does not fit right. In any of these cases, the fitter or tailor will measure, take in or let out seams, shorten, lengthen, cut, stitch, glue, or patch. The person doing the fitting should never be without a kit carrying as many tools and supplies as might be needed, including:

- Needles (different sizes)

- Thread (including embroidery thread)

- Safety pins

- Fabric glue

- A sharpie, tailor's chalk, or dressmaker's pencil

- Measuring tapes

- Variety of scissors

- Toupee tape (used to glue on hairpieces and mustaches)

- Camera

Rehearsal Reports

After rehearsals, the director may provide each department with a daily rehearsal report. The report details any changes made in the script that affect the department. The costume designer may get a report requesting additional costumes, accessories, or modifications. A rehearsal report could include such items as:

- Script change in movement (e.g., a character in a hoop skirt will now fall to the floor)

- New costume (e.g., replace winter hat with ear muffs)

- Accommodate items that are handled and stored (e.g., a cook uses a wooden spoon, so the cook's apron needs a large front pocket)

- Cuts or additions of accessories or props

- Requests to further distress a garment (e.g., a character gets bloodied)

Hair and Makeup

In many productions, the costume designer oversees makeup and hair. Makeup and hair designers collaborate with the costume designer to be consistent with the look and feel of the rest of the production. Designers review how each character's personality or age changes over the course of the play. The right hair and makeup also sends out visual cues to the audience about changes in the characters' circumstances, such as success, failure, wealth, poverty, happiness, or loss. Hair and makeup create the characters' attributes—beautiful or ugly, lively or dull, earnest or deceitful, healthy or sick, realistic or otherworldly.

The costume designer conceives the makeup design. Traditionally, professional stage actors take responsibility for their own makeup unless they have a character with a complicated makeup design, such as a werewolf. Nonprofessional actors, such as those in high school, may need more help. In theater, makeup has three purposes: to highlight the actor's features and expressions; to help the actor create a character; and for corrective purposes. Under the glare of lights, the actors' faces become washed out. In order to be visible to a large audience in a big theater, actors will apply their makeup heavily. In smaller venues, the actors' makeup will be more natural in appearance. All stage actors wear at least some makeup, generally a base color, powder, eyeliner, lipstick, and rouge. Makeup is also used to create a character. It can be used to portray age or disposition, such as funny, mean spirited, or larger than life. In creating characters from historical periods or from different countries, the costume designer looks at how different people regarded beauty. For example, a beautiful person in a different time or place could be one to have thin eyebrows, heavily made-up eyes, a heart-shaped mouth, or high cheekbones. Creating a character is not just about beauty; many characters require special effects to achieve their look, such as making a pointed chin out of plastic putty for the Wicked Witch of the West in *The Wizard of Oz* or creating disfigurements such as bruises, scars, or warts. Corrective makeup is makeup applied to make an actor look his or her very best. Corrective makeup uses special makeup formulas to achieve distinctive shadowing and highlighting of the actor's face. The costume designer, or sometimes the makeup designer under the direction of the costume designer, will draft a makeup plot. The makeup plot is a guide for each actor on how to apply his or her makeup and what it should look like. The makeup plot also juxtaposes each actor to one another to see how they relate. A minor character should not wear makeup that upstages a major character.

The costume designer also creates the hair designs. Most theater companies will employ a hair stylist whom the costume director will oversee. The costume director designs or requests beards, moustaches, wigs, and hairpieces, as well as deciding how natural hair will be worn. The designer chooses the color and the arrangement of the hair and decides when and if a hairstyle should be changed during the course of the play to reflect a change in the character.

The Production Phase

Budgets and the size of the productions vary, so the responsibilities of the costume designer during the production phase of a play also vary. In some instances, the costume designer is very hands-on during the production; other times, the work is delegated to others. Regardless of whether the costume designer is backstage helping the cast apply makeup or is standing in the wings taking notes, the costume designer is ultimately responsible for last minute costume preparations, costume handling, wardrobe organization, and arranging for someone to assist actors and oversee hair and makeup.

The phrase "**load-in**" is used to describe the day that all sets, lighting, sound equipment, costumes, and props are brought into the theater. It usually takes place within a week of opening night. All cast and staff are required for load-in. Each department has a scheduled time to arrive, and even with a schedule, it is an exceedingly hectic day. The costume department's load-in includes all costumes, garment racks, changing booths, props, and hair and makeup supplies. The costume designer discusses with the wardrobe staff how each costume should be handled and where each item should be stored. The wardrobe staff is instructed on how to put the garments on, as well as how to clean and launder them. The costume designer's costume plot is used as a check-in for inventory.

The week leading up to the opening performance is very fast paced, and a successful theater troupe handles the frenzied atmosphere with good organization. During the production "build/rehearsal" period, the costume designer has many obligations. The costume designer attends all the production meetings held by the director and the rest of the company. There are many rehearsals scheduled prior to the opening, and although the costume designer does not need to attend all, he or she must attend all **dress rehearsals** (that is, when the cast rehearses in costume, hair, and makeup) and should attend as many tech rehearsals as possible. For the costume designer, the tech rehearsals' focus is how lighting affects the costumes. Before the first dress rehearsal begins, most costume designers hold a **dress parade,** where, without the distraction of rehearsals, the actors parade on stage wearing their costumes. This allows the director, and the costume and wardrobe staff to get the full effect of the costumes, how they relate to the play, and how the group of actors will look together.

Postproduction

Strike is the last night of the performance, when the entire cast and crew tear down the set, pack the wardrobe, and clean up backstage. The costume designer's responsibility is to prepare the wardrobe for cleaning and storage and to separate out and pack rented costumes in their original bags for return as soon as possible. Props, makeup, and hair accessories should be sorted and packed up, and the clothing racks, dressing booths, and makeup and hairstyling tables and mirrors are packed and put on the theater's loading dock or area. It is a very hectic time, and safety is often an issue. But once the task is completed, everyone can head for the cast party.

Backstage, the costume and wardrobe staff must create order out of chaos.

CHAPTER FOUR

REALITY CHECK

There is likely no costume designer anywhere who is not wildly enthusiastic about his or her job. That is not to say that there is not a downside to costume designing. "Costume design isn't all glamour and frippery and shopping expeditions," says costume designer Deborah Hopper. In fact, many days can be mundane and decidedly unglamorous, such as waiting forever in line at a department store trying to return all the garments that did not work out, or being faced with a roomful of dirty rental costumes that must be quickly cleaned and examined before shipping back. As costume designer Vin Burnham puts it, "The 'slog' element is all part and parcel of the job. ... The good thing is, every day will be different. Take the rough with the smooth."

Under the Radar

"The work of a costume designer is backbreaking, never ending and, with the exception of awards season, usually uncelebrated," says costume designer Cherise Luter. Costume designers often go unrecognized, in comparison with the attention given to actors, directors, and producers. Oddly, many well-known costume designers prefer to have their work go unnoticed. Edith Head once said, "My motto is that the audience should notice the actors, not the clothes." Costume designer Tyler Kinney of Boston agrees that costume designers and their work often get overlooked. He says, "The director and the set designer will always be mentioned, and it is 50–50, I would say, as to whether the costume designer is mentioned. I never know if that's a good thing; I take it most of the time as a good thing, because my main job as a costume designer is to make the appropriate choices and not to distract from the language or the story telling, but to enhance it. Sometimes, if my work slips under the radar, I will take that as a job well done." Although many say an audience should not be distracted from the story by the costumes, it can nonetheless be upsetting to work so hard and yet go unnoticed.

Budget

People are attracted to costume design in order to express their creative and artistic talents. However, being creative is not the whole story, and in many ways costume design is a very practical job. A lively imagination is a necessary skill, of course, but so is being able to manage a budget and stick to a schedule. By virtue of being in a creative atmosphere and working with other creative people, it is wise to be patient and flexible. Costume designers all seem to say that nothing ever happens when it is supposed to and things change all the time. One of the biggest problems with unpredictability is having to work with a tight budget.

While there are numerous large and well-funded theater companies where costume designers' budgets are more generous, most high school and community theater companies operate with very tight budgets. When producers reduce small budgets even more, it is often the costume designer's budget that is one of the first to get cut. After all, rights fees for the plays can't be changed, and costs for the printing of programs, tickets, and promotional items are fixed.

Leaving actors or other inexperienced people in charge of costumes can lead to some costuming disasters. Sometimes when the budget is cut back, theater companies try to save money by hiring a costume designer at the last minute, giving the designer no time to absorb the script or get to know the characters well before going to work. "A costume designer's responsibilities in pre-production are so much more than most people," says director Raz Cunningham. As costume designer Patricia Dane points out, "So what do you do if you have a limited budget? You do the best you can!"

Challenges

When the costume design calls for mind-boggling costumes, costume designers must use their technical abilities along with their imagination. Tony Award–winning costume designer William Ivey Long has amazed audiences as well as other costume designers for his work on a theater production of *Cinderella*. The script called for Cinderella to change from her dirty rags into her ball gown on stage with no blackout. The costume change in front of a live audience was a huge challenge, and Ivey's ingenuity has left people marveling. He designed the costume so that the ball gown was intricately folded inside the dress of rags and Cinderella's hair and crown were hidden under her dirty scarf and wig. As the actress spun around under her fairy godmother's magic wand, she unwrapped and unfolded the ball gown hidden in her ragged dress. She pulled off the scarf and wig and stowed it under her ball gown, all in just the moments it took to spin around once. (To see the change, visit https://www.youtube.com/watch?v=9R2SHKtRBYg.)

All costume designers will face challenging costume requests, although high school productions will not require the sort of design challenges faced by Long. Costume designer Alyce Gilbert laments that young and/or new authors write plays that are more like movies, which means that scenes jump back and forth in time and more costume changes have to be done faster and more often. She says, "Years ago, actors had the time to go to their dressing rooms to change costumes between scenes. Now they cannot." Costume designer Long comments on the same challenge: "A quick change is four seconds. A fast change is, like, fifteen seconds. If you have a whole minute … a minute is, like, glorious." To accomplish these rapid costume changes, costume designers must make use of what is known as **costume rigging**, using special hidden fasteners, wires, magnets, pull strings, and more. Many elaborate period costumes are designed to be walked into because rushing a gown over an actor's head will muss up hair and makeup. Likewise, costume designers have to design

Dressers help actors make quick costume changes.

pants to be walked into in order to avoid the actor's shoes getting stuck inside.

Let's All Get Along

"People are not always at their best under extreme pressure and stressful conditions or when they are exhausted. The work can sometimes push people to their limits, so you will doubtless encounter tempers and irrational behavior when the heat is on, usually when there is no time left and still mountains to move. It happens on every job," warns costume designer Vin Burnham.

The Crew

In the frantic final weeks and days of a production, there is always so much to do. Everyone tries to do their part, but many have difficulty staying on schedule—especially if there are classes to go to and homework to be done. This only upsets someone else's schedule. What this means for a costume designer is that much of the last-minute details—sewing, embellishing, cleaning, repairing, altering, fitting, renting, shopping, and more—fall to him or her. Any student volunteering for the high school play should be prepared to do all of these tasks.

Many designers say that when it comes to schedule changes, the costume department is rarely accommodated. Fortunately, most costume designers know their way around the costume shop and wardrobe and can do many of the last-minute tasks themselves. In the weeks leading up to opening night, a costume designer can expect to put in very long hours, often working every day. School projects should be completed weeks before any scheduled performance. Designers must arrive before the actors to prepare for them and then leave after the actors to collect the costumes, inspect them for damage, repair them if necessary, clean them, check them against the inventory, and store them in their designated places for the next day.

Higher Ups

One of the more frustrating relationships costume designers can have is with producers and others who want to have a say in how the costumes should be designed. Very often this "design by committee" occurs in period productions. Everyone seems to have an opinion of what the historical costumes should look like, and producers and those providing money have a stake in the play's success. Many costume designers feel that each historic production should not be an exact recreation of one in the past but rather should have a fresh interpretation. Sometimes it is hard convincing the boss. Costume designers have a heavier workload with period productions. It is a challenge to engage modern theatergoers with plays set in the distant past. Costume designers make every effort to design period costumes that give an impression of the period, while making the costumes seem familiar enough that a present day audience can focus on the character and not the clothing.

Actors

Costume designers all have a favorite story about the challenges of working with actors. While some actors are appreciative and cooperative, some raise objections about the costume, and costume designers must either reach a compromise, concede, or as a last resort, call in the director to decide. Costume designers emphasize that they are making costumes for the character and not for the actor, meanwhile reassuring the actors that they do not want to dress them in uncomfortable, inappropriate, or ill-fitting clothes.

There are many ways actors can irk costume designers. For the most part, actors are considerate, but some are not. Some of their aggravating behaviors are:

- Showing up for fittings dirty or wearing strong perfume or cologne. Not only does it soil the costume, but costume designers spend hours in very close proximity to an actor when fitting and modifying his or her costumes.

- Not showing up on time or scheduling enough time for fittings.

- Removing tags from purchased garments before final decisions can be made, preventing the costume designer from returning the item.

- Altering or changing a hairstyle or facial hair without consulting the costume designer.

- Insisting on wearing their own clothes.

- Waiting to take issue with a costume until the last minute, leaving the costume designer scrambling to adjust the costume.

- Not telling the costume designer in a timely fashion about any damage or malfunction of a costume—broken zipper, rip in seam, lost buttons, hem coming undone, etc.

- Not bothering to account for all their costumes, jewelry, props, and accessories before leaving for the night.

- Going straight to the director with a costume problem, rather than speaking with the costume designer first.

- Insisting a costume will not work before trying it on and letting the costume designer make an assessment.

Taking the Heat

Every actor has a "most embarrassing moment on stage," and often it can be because of a costume malfunction. So, in effect, the costume designer has a "most embarrassing moment on stage" as well. One actor described her moment: "But, what happens when you look down, and realize something with your costume has gone wrong, terribly wrong? That magical moment turns into horror. Do you scream and run off stage?" Well, in this actor's case, it was her skirt. She was in a production with other dancers, and her skirt kept falling down. Every time she moved her arms she surreptitiously tugged at her skirt. At last she thought she had the problem solved by stepping behind a taller actor and yanking her skirt up. But once she came offstage, she realized she had tucked the back of her skirt inside of her tights, and not only that, but her tights had a hole which grew larger with every step. Of course she was mortified. But so was the costume designer.

Every costume designer has had costume snafus, such as this ill-fitting crown.

CRY FOR ME, ARGENTINA

The Tony Award–winning musical *Evita* is about the short life of Eva Peron, the beloved wife of the president of Argentina who dedicated herself to helping the poor.

The play, starring Patti LuPone, had a long run on Broadway. One day, LuPone was unable to perform,

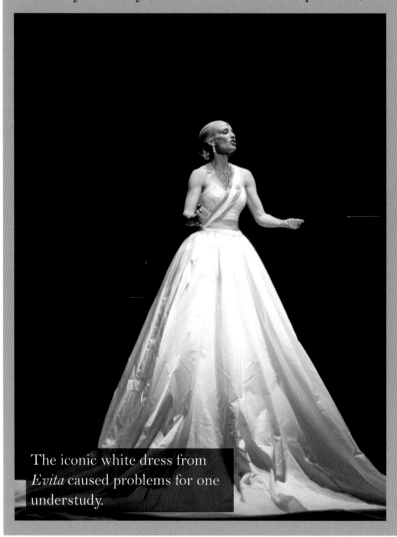

The iconic white dress from *Evita* caused problems for one understudy.

and her understudy, Nancy Opel, would play the role. Opel's first performance was a matinee, and the show went perfectly. However, no one warned Opel that there was a thick bundle of wires running across the back of the stage. During her first evening performance, after Opel finished singing the tearful theme song, "Don't Cry for me, Argentina," she crossed the stage in her elegant white dress with its enormous hoop skirt and tripped over the wires. Opel crumpled to the stage in a heap. The overly stiff, non-collapsible hoop skirt prevented her feet from reaching the floor and she could not get up. She lay there writhing like a bug flipped upside down. But the show must go on, and the other actor onstage began singing his song, whose lyrics ironically were:

> *High flying, adored, did you believe*
> *in your wildest moments all this would*
> *be yours?*
>
> *Stars in your eyes ... don't look down,*
> *it's a long, long way to fall.*
>
> *High flying, adored, what happens now,*
> *where do you go from here?*
>
> *For someone on top of the world, the view*
> *is not exactly clear.*

Eventually, Opel got to her feet and ad-libbed a line about suddenly becoming ill.

A costume designer takes the fall for something such as this. Although the actor was embarrassed in front of a live audience, the costume designer cringed inside as she questioned herself: Did she inspect the garment for the right measurement? What about the hole in the stocking? Was that there before the performance? It is the responsibility of a costume designer to prevent costume disasters such as this incident. But the beauty of theater is that everyone really is in it together. Once the embarrassment falls away there are lessons learned. The actor learned that she was resourceful and the costume designer learned to be more thorough about fitting the costume to the actor and being more aware of the conditions of the costume. As they say in the performing arts, "It's not how you fall, it's how you get up."

Family and Friends

Actor Kerry Hishon describes life in the theater and how it affects her personal life: "Not least of all, are the long hours and time away from my family, the drama, the stress … sometimes I wonder why on earth I do theatre. I have gone weeks at a time where I hardly see my husband, the house becomes a disaster area, I'm exhausted and I run out of clean clothes and fresh groceries. Yet despite all that, I still do theatre!"

The pace for a costume designer during a production is almost nonstop, especially as the final days draw near. During productions, costume designers and the rest of the cast and crew are dismayed at the lack of available time left over for family, friends, and social activities.

The Blues

When the curtain closes after the final call, everyone—actors, technicians, designers, directors, and all the members of the crew—feel an enormous letdown. The theater is empty and there is no reason to jump out of bed early the next morning. Cast and crew alike feel a melancholy after working so hard together, for so long, and with so much enthusiasm. They have bonded so closely during the play's production and then suddenly it all just … stops.

Many people in the theater say that they are seriously depressed for some time after a play ends. It is a natural response to having lost something so vital and so involving. Many cast and crew members cope by recognizing the strategies that can help them. For costume designers, the weight of all the scheduling, designing, discussing, fabricating, shopping, renting, and tending to hundreds of details is now gone. The smart move is to take a deep breath and enjoy a sense of relief from all the responsibility. Some costume designers say they feel pangs of regret for costumes they think they may have made too hurriedly or were the wrong color, shape, or just did not suit the character well enough. People in the business say "relax"—the audience surely did not notice, especially for a high school show with a limited budget, and the costume designer certainly gave his or her all to the production. Loneliness is a big part of the postproduction blues. The costume designer is part of a group of people who worked very closely together and had formed a unique bond. The costume designer, through fittings and discussions about costumes, spent many long hours with each cast member individually and worked side by side with the backstage crew.

Maintaining friendships with non-theater friends and seeking them out after the play is over helps reduce loneliness. Many theater companies wait to have a cast party for a week or two after the show closes and all the excitement (and the letdown) has settled. The cast party is a great way to share the ups and downs of the experience and find closure, all the while strengthening the bond with the "theater family." A cast party makes it easier for everybody to move on.

Theater Etiquette

People in the theater share a code of ethics, or theater etiquette. It is an essential survival tool to be courteous with people who work closely together under multiple deadlines and have different roles and individual responsibilities. The success of any production relies on the cast and crew showing respect for each other's talents, time schedules, work, and creativity. Some etiquette rules to follow:

- Be on time.

- Forego all social activities that interfere with the production schedule and personal workload.

- Always inform the director in advance of an important prior commitment.

- Do not leave the theater without the director or someone in the costume or wardrobe department knowing.

- Never criticize a cast or crew member.

- Accept both praise and constructive criticism gracefully.

- Take good care of stage properties and costume shop tools.

- Refrain from saying anything that might be misconstrued as insulting when fitting an actor. (e.g., "Your legs are too short for these pants, we will have to hem them.")

- Remember everyone has a schedule and do not interrupt or interfere with others' time management.

- Limit socializing.

- After watching rehearsals, give any costume notes to the actor, not just the director or wardrobe manager.

- Always have a planner, sketchbook, and pencils at the ready.

- Do not move or borrow props or tools.

- Always be gracious.

CAD software makes costume design changes fast and easy.

CHAPTER FIVE

ONE FOR ALL

On the stage and behind the scenes, theater workers blend their many and various talents. Through their love of theater and their "creative gene," theater people share many similar characteristics. Yet they each have individual skills and duties that are quite diverse. The skills learned in your high school or community theater can be applied to professions outside the theater.

New Directions

Costume designers and other members of the theater world who may want to look for a different way to make a living have plenty of valuable skills to take with them into other careers. There are numerous options in business, where theater-trained skills including scheduling, managing, budgeting, and communicating are highly desired. Persons may find employment as event planners, management trainers, marketing executives, or as educators in public speaking or communication techniques. Many companies have corporate retreats, and their executives have hired actors and other theater people to provide guidance and inspiration to their employees in subject areas such as teamwork, effective human relations and communication skills, grace under pressure, and strategies for meeting deadlines. Many theater people have also been successful as entrepreneurs, taking their specialized talents, such as creativity and commitment, into the marketplace themselves. Many costume designers, for example, have started a clothing line and/or opened a fashion boutique.

Training in theater gives people an advantage in other professions as well. Particularly in their experience in public speaking and with their dedication, self-discipline, willingness to work long hours, willingness to listen and interact with empathy, and attention to detail, theater-trained people can also be successful as lawyers, educators, and politicians. There is a relatively new field of law called fashion law whose lawyers represent clients in many aspects of the business of fashion, including intellectual property, business negotiations, finance, international trade, and government regulation.

Art and Tech

Although many costume designers prefer doing sketches and renderings by hand, a growing number are also using, to some degree, computers. "It is especially helpful when we need to check to see how a garment was worn in a given scene, rather than tracking down [notes], we can just look online. Also, when characters are added to a scene, a location changes, a character is deleted, or a new scene is added, with a few simple keystrokes, the information can be updated. I like the fact that there is new technology aspiring to help me and other designers, while at the same time creating new opportunities for costume designers," says costume designer Jeremy Eagan. Computer-aided design is becoming the future in the fashion industry and in costume design. A costume designer's knowledge of CAD software can translate into many other career paths.

Many members of the various technical departments of the theater—sound and lighting designers and engineers, electricians, and technical directors—are sought-after employees in tech-related jobs. The technicians not only have technology skills, but they have experience in working under pressure and being analytical, flexible, and capable of meeting deadlines.

Costume Designers Forge New Careers

Some costume designers move on to other careers, most of them related to their artistic backgrounds. Some of the most common new careers are in fashion design and retail clothing sales. Another important and often well-paid field is event planning. Costume designers can be well suited to this work. An event planner coordinates meetings, conventions, and special events, such as weddings and fundraisers. The job requires imagination, an eye for detail, good customer relations, budget consciousness, the ability to meet deadlines, and the willingness to work long hours on an irregular schedule.

Other jobs include working on displays for department stores and museums, managing

Edith Head once said, "What a costume designer does is a cross between magic and camouflage."

HEAD OF HER CLASS

There is a favorite anecdote in the costume design world about Edith Head, who is considered by many to be the most famous and highly regarded costume designer of all time. After graduating with a degree in French art and literature from Stanford University, she was hired to teach French at a private girls' school. The father of two of her students was Cecil B. DeMille, the head of Paramount Pictures. On a trip to the studio with her students, Head fell in love with the wardrobe and costume department and decided to apply for a job. She could not draw and actually submitted artwork done by her students.

After she got the job, she immediately confessed to her new boss that she did not know how to draw. Her boss replied, "You had better learn then!" Head's first big break was designing costumes for Mae West and Cary Grant in the film *She Done Him Wrong*. Her outrageous costumes for Mae West impressed everyone in the business. She became highly sought after as a costume designer, and one of her special skills was creating costume boards for each scene and each actor.

Head won eight Academy Awards. She was the first female head designer at a major studio and worked with legendary actors and directors such as Alfred Hitchcock, Marilyn Monroe, Audrey Hepburn, Elizabeth Taylor, Paul Newman, Steve Martin, and Robert Redford. She was, and still is, an inspiration to all in the field of costume design.

department stores and boutiques, and being a clothing or jewelry buyer for a retail store. Costume designers are ideal employees for managing a retail clothing or jewelry store. They create appealing displays, produce effective promotions and advertisements, and interact effectively with wholesalers, associates, and customers.

But while there are numerous other professions costume designers are prepared to do, many would not give up their career in theater for anything in the world. Costume designers are essential in bringing theater art to life. As actor Tom Wilkinson said, "I once did a role which I couldn't rehearse in my street clothes. I had to have the character's costume on before I could rehearse it. I just couldn't think as the character unless I looked like him."

Shared Traits

A background in theater is excellent preparation for countless other careers. While those who work in theater love their work, many also acknowledge that it is a very competitive field, has very irregular work schedules, and does not necessarily pay well. Many choose to work in theater part time and maintain other careers that give their lives more balance and earn them a greater income. Fortunately, theater skills can take people far in other career directions. People with a background in theater learn valuable skills that can put them in good stead to also become lawyers, politicians, business executives, educators, computer technicians, electricians, and more.

People in theater, no matter what their roles in the production may be—literary, musical, managerial, artistic, or technical—all can provide substantial benefits to future employers. To begin with, theater people know how to start a major project and follow through to a successful finish. They know how to interact in close, day-to-day situations with a wide variety of personality types—outgoing, intense, serious, practical, idealist, introverted, egotistic, energetic, and more. Theater people coordinate with each other's departments, such as lighting engineers with choreographers, or costume designers with set designers. They coordinate their production responsibilities and manage their schedules under deadline pressures and the commotion of everyone working in the same physical space.

Each individual in a theater production has a certain assignment, and each must take responsibility for his or her own work and be ultimately accountable for it. A malfunction in a costume, for example, can have its root in the design, in the construction, in the fitting, or even because the actor mishandled the costume. However,

Training in costume design can lend itself to careers in other fields such as fashion design, advertising, and event planning.

no matter what, how, or who damaged the costume, it is the responsibility of the costume designer to repair, replace, or redesign to make everything right. The costume designer and everyone else in the theater company are accountable for their work within the production. They waste no time on blame or excuses because the "show must go on."

Theater people are also aware that there is a code of ethics and a set of rules to follow. Nothing would be accomplished in the short time it takes for so many disparate parts to come together without some form of order. Everyone in each department communicates and takes direction from the head of each department, and every department head takes direction from the director. A respect for authority is paramount.

For many theater people, especially actors, directors, and designers, envisioning the big picture comes naturally. In many businesses or organizations, there are certain people who are tasked with envisioning an idea or inventing a product, while others in the organization are assigned to produce it. In the theater, the creative, visionary, and inventive people are also the same people who physically, technically, and intellectually turn the vision into a finished piece of work.

All in all, the qualities of people who work in theater are desirable to employers. The qualities can also help people with a theater background become successful entrepreneurs. Theater people share common traits, such as energy, fortitude, enthusiasm, and an ability to work under pressure. They also have good organization and communication skills and know how to work as a team. Some of the most important qualities are self-confidence, self-discipline, and determination. Every play starts from zero and goes forward, collecting and combining people, ideas, and resources along the way until one day, without fail, a completed production is the result. All the people involved in the production have the confidence to know they will get to the end, the self-discipline to learn their role or accomplish their tasks, and the determination to do so despite conflicts, crashes, and challenges. In a nutshell, theater people have developed these natural and learned traits, qualities, and abilities:

- Communication skills

- Problem-solving abilities

- Ability to work independently

- Ability to work as a team

- Time-budgeting skills

- Promptness

- Respect for deadlines

- Accepting authority

- Flexibility

- Self-discipline

- Accountability

- Self-confidence

- Determination

- Commitment

All of these can carry someone a long way.

GLOSSARY

baste To sew fabric pieces together with long or loose temporary stitches.

breaking down A term used to describe making a fabric look aged, worn, or used.

built Term used to describe how a costume is constructed.

costume craft artisans Persons working in a costume department who craft accessories and special wardrobe pieces such as masks, jewelry, helmets, and fringe.

costume plot A list outlining which characters appear in which scene and what they are wearing.

costume rigging Techniques for building a costume to be easily changed into or out of.

creative team The group of theatrical collaborators, such as the director, designers, and choreographer, who make the creative choices.

croquis A sketch of a human form used to draw rough preliminary costume designs.

distress The process of aging a garment so the items no longer look new; a synonym for breaking down.

draping Creating a pattern by draping muslin on a dress form, pinning and tucking to get the desired shape, and transferring that shape to craft paper.

dress parade Designated time when the costumes are worn by the actors under stage lights in order for the director and costume designer to make any necessary changes or improvements to the costumes.

dress rehearsal A rehearsal for which actors are dressed in their costumes.

fitter A person who adjusts and alters a garment for a particular person.

load-in The act of bringing into the theater all the sound and lighting equipment, costumes, scenery, stage properties, and props.

look books A set of photographs displaying a costume designer's costumes.

mood boards An arrangement of images, swatches, pieces of text, and renderings, intended to evoke the look and feel of the costume designs.

rendering A perspective drawing of a design.

stitcher A person who sews.

strike The act of dismantling and packing away the set, sound and lighting equipment, wardrobe, props, and stage properties after the last performance.

swatch A sample piece of fabric.

tear sheet A collection of photographs and illustrations torn out of magazines that are early ideas for a costume.

textile A fabric that is woven or knit.

texture The structure formed by the threads of a fabric.

Tony Award Award that honors achievement in Broadway theater. An Academy Award for the stage.

trim Details added to garments either by hand or machine, such as braids, buttons, embroidery, lace edgings, piping, ribbons, ruffles or tassels.

FOR MORE INFORMATION

Books

Cleveland, Annie O. *Digital Costume Design &
Rendering: Pens, Pixels, and Paint.* New York:
Costume and Fashion Press, 2014.

Cunningham, Rebecca. *Basic Sewing for Costume
Construction: A Handbook.* Long Grove, IL:
Waveland Press, 2005.

Koda, Harold. *100 Dresses.* New York: Metropolitan
Museum of Art, 2010.

Leventon, Melissa. *What People Wore When: A Complete
Illustrated History of Costume from Ancient Times
to the Nineteenth Century for Every Level of Society.*
New York: St. Martin's Griffin, 2008.

Tan, Huaixiang. *Character Costume Figure Drawing:
Step-by-Step Drawing Methods for Theatre Costume
Designers.* Burlington, MA: Focal Press, 2013.

Wolfe, Brian, Nick Wolfe. *Extreme Costume Makeup:
25 Creepy and Cool Step-by-Step Demos.* Cincinnati,
OH: IMPACT Books, 2013.

Websites

The American Association of Community Theater
The Costume Designer's Job
http://www.aact.org/costume-designer
Among the many articles on the different positions
that put on a production is this glance at the costume
designer's job.

Costume Designers Guild
The Costume Designer
http://costumedesignersguild.com/magazine/
This website is the online magazine of the Costume
Designers Guild.

***Threads* Magazine**
http://www.threadsmagazine.com
This online magazine provides articles on sewing for
the beginner to the expert.

Victoria and Albert Museum
Designing Stage Costumes
http://www.vam.ac.uk/content/articles/d/designing-
stage-costumes
Take a look at thousands of costumes that are on
display at this museum in London.

Videos

Arts Insight: Theatre Costumes
http://video.houstonpbs.org/video/2365612517
Houston Public Media provides a glance into the
construction of costumes for the theater.

**Backstage at the Met Opera's Costume Shop:
Frenzy, Fabric and Velvet Codpieces**
https://www.youtube.com/watch?v=-gKL60SPWf4_
Elissa Iberti explains what she needs to do to oversee
the preparation of eight hundred costumes for five
productions at once.

Costumes, Wigs, Makeup at the National Theatre
https://www.youtube.com/watch?v=aLROmAKAUyo
Find out how the National Theatre's costume
department works and what skills are needed to create
a world onstage.

INDEX

ABOUT THE AUTHOR

Ruth Bjorklund lives on Bainbridge Island, Washington. The author of numerous books, she has a master's degree in library and information science from the University of Washington. A versatile author, she has written books on subjects as diverse as state history, world cultures, and the internment of Japanese Americans during World War II.